Walki

CERED

COAST

A guide to the coastal path from Cardigan to Borth

Liz Allan

Illustrated by Lynne Denman

Cover photographs by Penny Sharp

KITTIWAKE

Published by:
Kittiwake
3 Glantwymyn Village Workshops, Glantwymyn,
Machynlleth, Montgomeryshire SY20 8LY

First edition 2000. Revised edition 2006. Reprints 2007, 2008.
New edition 2009.

Printed by MWL, Pontypool.

A catalogue record for this book may be found at the British Library.

ISBN: 978 1 902302 67 6

INTRODUCTION

The original version of this book was first written in 2000 when there was no continuous coast-path along the glorious Ceredigion coastline. It was inspired by the many weekends spent exploring the delights of the long distance coastal path in my neighbouring Pembrokeshire. As I explored that splendid county I mused that, if I could walk the length of the Pembrokeshire coast, why could I not do the same in my home county of Ceredigion with its equally spectacular coastline? Well, I am very happy to say that in 2008 the **Ceredigion Coast Path** was finally opened and there are some lovely new stretches of coastline just waiting to be explored by both visitor and locals alike. There is something very special about discovering new paths along coastline previously only seen from sea. It presents entirely new perspectives.

The route is an adventure. A challenge in parts, and easy as pie in others. It has been divided up into six sections – each representing a day's walking ending in a village or town with accommodation and refreshment. Each of these settlements is served by a regular bus service, (but check times, particularly if walking in the winter), so the walk can also be done in individual sections. I do hope, though, that you will be able to find a week of your holidays to discover the whole of this relatively unexplored part of the Welsh coastline. With its internationally important marine wildlife, stunning landscapes, picturesque villages and warm welcomes, I'm sure you will not be disappointed.

During recent summers, the *Cardi Bach*, a bus service particularly aimed for walkers, operated from New Quay to Cardigan visiting the many coastal villages and towns en route. It is hoped to continue to operate *Cardi Bach* in future years.

About the author:
Liz Allan was born in South Wales where she spent most of her child-
hood exploring the Gower coast through play. Having lived and worked in
Australia and London, she now lives in New Quay in Ceredigion. She has
worked for Ceredigion County Council since 1992 as their Conservation
Management Officer. She has an MSc in Protected Landscape Management
from the University of Wales, Aberystwyth and believes strongly in both the
conservation and enjoyment of our natural environment.

About the illustrator:
Lynne Denman was born and raised near the sea in Somerset and Jersey. She
learned to love the mountains, too, when the family moved to the north of
England. She married a Welshman and found all her favourite landscapes
together in West Wales, along with an ancient language and lively culture
thrown into the bargain. She is a practising artist and exhibition designer,
working mostly in the field of local and natural history.

Photography by:
Penny Sharp, originally from Yorkshire, but now a local photographer who
specialises in land and seascapes.

Contents

Cardigan to Aberporth

11.7 miles/18.7 kilometres

Cardigan to Mwnt

6.4 miles/10.2 kilometres

Cardigan – the gateway to Ceredigion – The ancient borough of Cardigan received its first charter in 1199 and was once considered to be the second most important port in Wales. The official start of the **Ceredigion Coast Path** is the bronze otter next to the bridge on the northern bank of the River Teifi. Cardigan Castle was built in 1110 and is the site of the first eisteddfod in 1176. Much of the original castle has long since gone but there is a big restoration project underway to repair the later mansion and grounds. Unfortunately, at the time of checking this route (January 2009), there were no coast footpath signs or way-markers at the start of the route in Cardigan to guide the way out of the town along the estuary to the sea.

With the bridge behind you and the castle grounds to your right, walk up the hill towards the town centre and turn first left at the road leading down the hill to Somerfields super market. Continue to the other end of the car-park and follow the path from the car-park near the floating Indian restaurant up the bank into the recreation ground. At the top, turn right and continue through the play area to where it meets the road. Continue along this road with the cemetery on your left and pass the entrance to the small Mwldan wood on your right until you reach a T-junction. Turn left along this road passing the Maes Radley playing fields on your left. This narrow lane winds and twists and passes a left-hand turning to 'Old Castle Farm'. Keep following this quiet lane until you arrive at the entrance to 'Rhos Fach' farm and the property 'Bryn a Mor'. There was no footpath sign at the field-gate and kissing gate (marked no. 12) on the right before this entrance in January 2009, nevertheless rest assured that the coastpath continues across the left hand side of the fields. The path emerges onto the road to Gwbert.

Turn left at the Gwbert road and walk along the pavement with the marvellous wide vista of theTeifi estuary on your left. Listen out for the curlew and oystercatchers, and watch for redshank and solitary herons. The pavement continues past the boat club and Patch Caravan Park until it reaches a panoramic car-parking viewing area. There are benches here and it is worth pausing to gaze southwards over the spectacular expanse of Poppit Sands and the Pembrokeshire coastline beyond..There is no pavement from now on so proceed with care following the road as it passes the Gwbert Hotel and the entrance to the Cliff Hotel, before it bears right and continues up the hill. At the time of writing the intended coastpath route beyond the Cardigan Island Farm Park was still under dispute, so the walker for the time being has to continue along the road until it reaches the village of Ferwig. Where the road bears to the right to pass through the village, turn left along a farm lane with an old 'No Through Road' sign. This lane passes by several farm buildings and a duck pond. Cross the cattle grid leading to 'Nantycroi Farm' that does B&B and has camping/touring facilities and enter the farm yard. A faded green man sign points to the left to a track leading to Mwnt.

Follow this track and enjoy the coastal views of Cardigan Island, which is now a nature reserve managed by the local Wildlife Trust. Puffins used to nest there, but rats wiped them out when they got onto the island from a ship that had been wrecked on the rocks. Efforts by the Wildlife Trust to re-introduce puffins to the island have, to date, proved unsuccessful. About 4000 pairs of lesser black-backed gulls now nest there. Where the track ends at a field gate, turn left

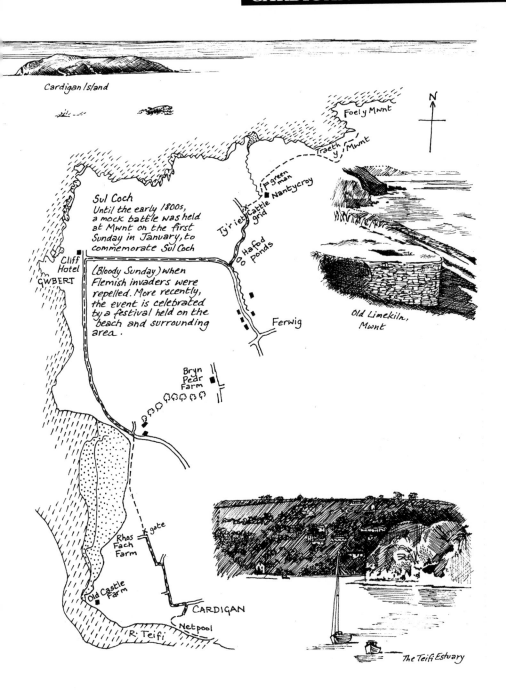

Cardigan Island

Foel y Mwnt

N

Traeth y Mwnt

green man

Nantycroy

Ty'riet

Cattle grid

Sul Coch
Until the early 1800s,
a mock battle was held
at Mwnt on the first
Sunday in January, to
commemorate Sul Coch

Hafod Ponds

Cliff
Hotel
GWBERT

(Bloody Sunday) when
Flemish invaders were
repelled. More recently,
the event is celebrated
by a festival held on the
beach and surrounding
area.

Ferwig

Old Limekiln,
Mwnt

Bryn
Pedr
Farm

gate

Rhos
Fach
Farm

Old Castle Farm

CARDIGAN

Netpool

R. Teifi

The Teifi Estuary

and follow the fence-bank to the kissing gate. Turn right onto the coastal path which leads you directly down into Mwnt. Some of the best displays of Spring Squill can be found on the long-abandoned arable fields along the cliff tops to the east.

The sheltered sandy cove, ideal for swimming, is a National Trust property. From the vantage point of the conical outcrop known as Foel y Mwnt, bottlenose dolphins, harbour porpoise and, more rarely, basking shark and sunfish can sometimes be seen close into shore. It's also an excellent spot to watch for choughs. The white-washed church at Mwnt would have been a pilgrim church on the route from St. David's in the south to Strata Florida and Bardsey off the Llyn Peninsula in North Wales. The church is believed to commemorate a battle in 1155 near here between the Norman Flemings and the Welsh.

How to get there:
Country lanes from Cardigan and Gwbert. Cardi Bach & bus services run to Cardigan.
Facilities: Toilets and take-away food (seasonal) Camping and B&B, National Trust Car park.
Features of interest: The old lime kiln, and the 14th century Church of the Holy Cross, with its 12th century font.

Llangranog is the birthplace of the County's most celebrated teacher of navigation - one 'Cranogwen', Sarah Jane Rees. Born in 1838 she acquired her master mariner's certificate and taught in the village school. She coached generations of local boys in the art of deep-sea navigation and died in 1916.

Llangrannog to New Quay
9.3 miles/14.9 kilometres

Llangranog to Cwmtudu
5.5 miles/8.8 kilometres

The coast path now is continuous all the way to Cwmtydu, thanks to an entirely new section of path that has been opened from the Urdd Centre. It passes some of the most spectacular scenery in Ceredigion.

Take the steps leaving the northern end of the beach, past the Patio café. The coastal path climbs towards Pen y Badell, an imposing Celtic Hill Fort. When you reach the gate directly in front of you, turn left along the track and circumnavigate the Hill Fort which is covered in purple heather and yellow gorse during summer. Listen for the sounds of chough, a blackbird like bird with red legs and beak, or the screech of the peregrine overhead. Looking down at the promontory, the small island of Ynys Lochtyn lies beneath you. This is a good place to watch for harbour porpoise and bottlenose dolphins feeding, or grey seals popping their heads above the waves.

The path continues around the side of the hill, before rising steeply and continuing north to follow the cliff top to the Urdd Centre with its' dry ski slope. This is one of two Urdd Gobaith Cymru (Welsh Youth Movement) centres and was established in 1932 offering over 20,000 youngsters a variety of activities throughout the year. At the Heritage Centre you can learn all about the history of Llangrannog and listen to tales from a master storyteller. It's worth leaving the path for, and it's open all year.

The coast-path bears left at Urdd Centre and the coast-path sign points the way ahead. Keeping the field fence on your right the path gradually descends to a kissing gate and the fine stone plinth which commemorates the official opening of the Ceredigion coast-path in the summer of 2008. The path continues across a field to a bridge with the sound of rushing water cascading over the cliffs below. During wet weather, there is considerable run-off from the fields and the path can be quite boggy until the next kissing gate is reached and you enter a field with the large sign asking you to keep your dog on the lead. Keep to the left of this field along the line of bent old hawthorn and blackthorn trees. The rocky stack close inshore provides a useful spot for cormorants drying their wings and digesting their latest meal.

The path gradually rises and looking ahead the new path climbs the gorse and bracken slope of Hirallt, the highest point along the Ceredigion coastline. Again one wonders at the ingenuity and sheer hard graft of creating the line of path here, as it cuts into the side of this stretch of dramatic slope with sheer tenacity. For us walkers, it provides us with a wonderful path to enjoy some really spectacular views ahead and behind. The path eventually turns inland and descends into the valley, emerging onto a lane adjacent to a house. Turn left and then left again at the staggered crossroads. Follow this road which continues to wind its way along the lovely wooded valley of Afon Ffynnon-Ddewi until you reach the small hamlet of Cwmtudu.

How to get there: Country lanes from A487 to Llwyndafydd. **Facilities:** Public toilets. Car parking. Take-away and café (seasonal). Camping. **Features of interest:** Restored lime kiln

Birds Rock

Cwm tudu *gate*

Castell Bach

FB

Pen -y- graig

Afon Soden

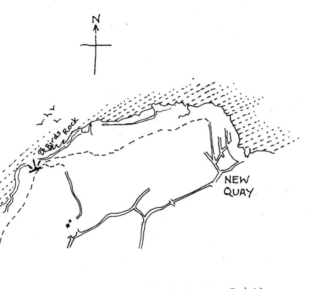

NEW QUAY

Cardigan Bay Bottlenose Dolphins

The population in the Bay of these fascinating marine mammals is estimated to be around 200 animals. Bottlenose dolphins can grow up to 4m. in length and live for 30 years or more. Adult females have one calf every two to three years during March to September and these young take 18 months or so to wean. If you spot two dorsal fins very close together, take a close look, as these are likely to be a mother with her calf.

Well defined coast path all the way, passing by secluded coves and wooded valleys.

The small cove of Cwmtydu is owned by the National Trust. The old lime kiln that is set back from the beach has been recently restored, and in their heyday kilns were used to burn limestone brought in by boat from Pembrokeshire. Farmers from the surrounding countryside would come by horse and cart to collect the lime for spreading on their fields as a fertiliser. This small cove and surrounding caves were also once used by smugglers bringing in goods such as French brandy and salt. The contraband was hidden in dark, secluded caves until it could safely be carried inland on horseback.

The rocks and caves just south of Cwmtydu are known locally as Seals Bay. There are estimated to be just over 4700 grey seals in the West Wales area and along this stretch of coastline approximately 17 seal pups are born every year between September to December. The grey seal can spend up to 80% of the time submerged when they are at sea looking for food, and they can stay underwater during a short dive for up to 8 minutes. They use Seals Bay to haul out onto the rocks to rest in between their feeding excursions.

From Cwmtydu, the coast-path leaves the cove from the kissing gate at the northern end of the beach. The gradual climb up gorse and bracken covered slopes brings you to a fine viewing point. Looking ahead, the remains of small earthen banks can be seen of the Iron Age promontory fort, Castell Bach. That was occupied from around the 3rd century BC for about 400 years by a small tribe of Celts. The path continues to the little sheltered cove at Cwm Soden down steps and over a bridge. The coast-path now turns left and then bears right to start climbing the slope, however, a short detour to the right from the bridge is recommended in the Spring as in the valley wood anemone, wild primrose, wood sorrel, bluebells abound alongside the Afon Soden with it's cascading mini-waterfall.

The coast-path to New Quay climbs once more and continues along the cliffs, descending at one point to pass through the sheltered area of Coybal with its steep slopes covered in blackthorn.

When you reach the white walled old coast-guard hut, now restored to the Cardigan Bay Lookout, keep an eye open for the most important seabird breeding colony in Ceredigion – Craig yr Adar (Birds Rock). Pass the lookout hut, and the path descends for a few metres until you reach a small quarried area. Spend a few moments here looking over the cliff, and from Spring to early summer you will be rewarded with the sight of nearly 3000 guillemots crammed onto the bare rock ledges. Razorbills, kittiwakes, fulmar, cormorants, shags and lesser black-backed gulls also breed here. This is also a good area to watch for seals. Continue along the well defined coast path through an interesting area of sub-maritime heath on uncultivated sea-cliff slopes at the headland above New Quay. The path emerges at Lewis Terrace, one of three fine terraces that overlook Cardigan Bay and give marvellous views on a clear day towards the Llyn Peninsula. Continue until you see a fingerpost on the left to a path leading behind some houses. This path emerges onto the middle terrace, Marine Terrace; turn left and continue down through the old quarry above the Fish Factory towards the stone harbour, built in 1836.

How to get there:
A486 from A487 at Synod Inn. B4324 from Llanarth. Buses from Aberystwyth and Cardigan.
Facilities: Car parking. Public toilets. Pubs. Cafés. Shops. PO. Bank. Accommodation. Tourist Information Centre (seasonal).
Features of interest: Wildlife boat trips, Cardigan Bay Boat Place, Heritage Centre. Cardigan Bay Marine Wildlife Centre – all seasonal.

New Quay to Llanrhystud
14 miles/22.5 kilometres

As well as some fine cliff-top walking, much of this section of the walk is along the beach and provides many an opportunity to study first hand the old cliff-line along the coast prior to the last Ice Age. The sediments deposited during that time and since are spectacularly displayed between New Quay and Cei Bach, and between Aberaeron and Aberarth.

New Quay to Aberaeron
6.5 miles/10.5 kilometres

Setting off on this next stretch of coastal path MUST coincide with low water, as this is the only possible way to walk along the beach Traeth Gwyn to Llanina Point. Check the times of the tides at the Harbourmaster's office on the Quay. Otherwise, you can walk up Glanmor Terrace from the harbour and turn left at the little alley immediately before the Black Lion pub. Continue until the path emerges onto the main road, the B4324 that leads to Llanarth, turn left and then left again down Brongwyn Lane. This lane leads you down to a mid point along Traeth Gwyn where it is possible to continue along the beach in albeit but the highest tides to Llanina point. Otherwise continue along the B4324 and turn left just beyond Quay West Caravan Park at the signpost to Cei Bach. If you take this route you will be following in famous footsteps, as it was along this lane that Dylan Thomas used to walk during his trips from his home at the bungalow, 'Majoda' to the various hostelries in New Quay, notably the Black Lion.

Ina, the 7th Century King of the West Saxons famous as the builder of Glastonbury Abbey, was supposedly shipwrecked at Llanina Point but was rescued by some local people. To show his gratitude, he built a church which is now said to be lost beneath the waves, but whose eerie bell can sometimes be still heard on dark, stormy nights. The present church just visible from the beach was built in 1850. At Llanina Point the stream is passable only during a dry spell, allowing you to carry on along the beach to Cei Bach where you leave the beach via the access track. Continue past the caravan park, car-park and pub to the t-junction. Continue straight ahead and turn left along the path that leads to the property 'Llwynon'.

If, however, you head for Cei Bach via the road, turn right at the t-junction that points left towards Cei Bach and the path is a few metres up on your left. The coastal path north to Aberaeron starts again here. Look to your left as you approach the property 'Llwynon' and follow the path leading into the copse. The path gently climbs again through wooded areas and open fields, up onto the open of the bracken covered slopes. Resist the temptation to follow any paths that lead away to the right. The path passes over a waterfall where the Afon Drwyi cascades into the sea and climbs again across the gorse-covered slope. The line of the coastal path would benefit from some sign-posting at this point as it has become quite confusing as the result of recently formed tracks from the nearby quad biking establishment and, one suspects, from people trying to make their way up the slope the best they can. Once at the top the path continues across bracken slopes, then farmland and finally along a track (wonderful for blackberry picking) to the holiday village at Gilfach yr Halen, which was formerly a dairy farm.

Pass through the yard alongside the building on your left and turn left down along the road. Keep following this road for about 500 metres until you see the signs on your left directing you across some fields back onto the coast-path. The coastal path now continues all the way to the colourful Georgian harbour town of Aberaeron.
/continues on page 20

How to get there:
A487 and A482. Bus service from Cardigan, Aberystwyth, Lampeter, Carmarthen.
Facilities: Car parking. Public toilets. Pubs.

Cafés. Shops. PO. Banks. Acccommodation. Tourist Information Centre.
Features of interest: Local craft centre. Vineyard.

New Quay Head

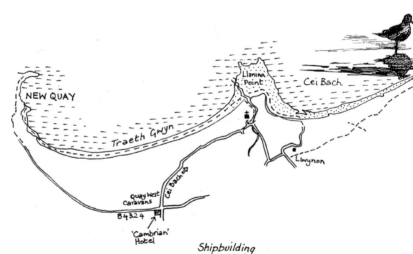

Shipbuilding

The great era of maritime history in the County peaked during the 19th century. New Quay was the most important shipbuilding centre with some 240 vessels being built at New Quay and Cei Bach between 1800-1882 by at least nine different builders. There are few signs left along the coast of this heyday, save for a few ruined limekilns and harbours that are now full of pleasure craft.

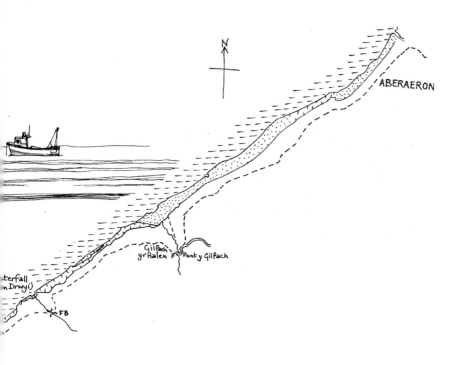

ABERAERON

Gilfach yr Halen

Pont y Gilfach

terfall
n Drwyi)

FB

New Quay

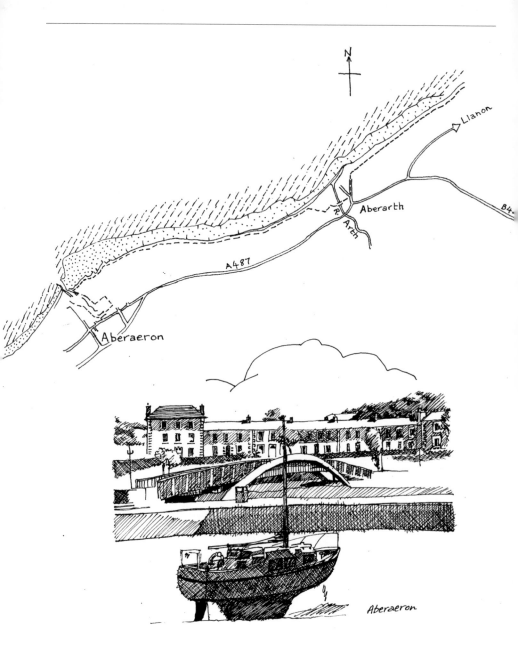

N

Llanon

Aberarth

R. Arth

B4

A487

Aberaeron

Aberaeron

Dolphins (not sharks!)

Aberaeron to Llanrhystud
7.4 miles/11.9 kilometres

The coastal path leaves the North beach car-park and continues along the shingle fore-shore and the edge of the low clay cliffs to the small quiet village of Aberarth, one of the earliest settlements along the Ceredigion coast. On the shore at low tide, clearly visible to the south of the village are the remains of large semi-circular walls of stone which are thought to date back to the 6th century. These walls are the remains of fish traps, stranding fish such as salmon, sprats and mullet as the tide went out.

Leave the rocky beach at Aberarth via the concrete steps and take the first left after a row of cottages. Follow this little village lane as it winds its way down to a bridge crossing the Arth river with its small waterfalls and deep pools. Crossing the bridge, turn left at the lane and take the next lane on the right marked with a 'green man' sign towards the access to the beach. At the end of this lane at the start of the path back to the beach, there is a field-gate on your right. This is the start of the coast-path to Llanrhystud. Through the field gate, continue up the slope and across the field to a kissing-gate. There has been bad erosion of these soft cliffs and the original line of the path was lost. As part of the Ceredigion Coastpath project a new path has been created to allow for this section of coast to be opened up again to walkers. Keep going straight ahead to a second kissing gate where an old track on the left leads the way ahead. This is a lovely old track bordered by blackthorn alongside the cliff-top and makes for very pleasant, gentle walking. Follow the directions of two coastpath posts and con-tinue along the path as it crosses over a small stream cascading down the cliffs. The path then begins its descent toward the sweep of Llanon beach. The path crosses two stiles and a tiny trickle of a stream (two stepping stones) and continues ahead across the field to a finger-post pointing right by another stream (this one is bigger but with no bridge, but passable). Cross over the stile that has an orange 'Tir Gofal' (Wales agri-environmen-tal scheme) way-marker sign and continue across several open flat fields to where the path emerges at the lane to the beach near Morfa Mawr Hotel and Restaurant.

There are now two options. Either, a short walk along the beach if the tide is favourable, to the steel steps and then along the quiet village lanes in the direction of the church. Or a right turn along the beach access lane to the main A487 road where you turn left and walk along the pavement for about 150 metres into Llanon village. Continue along the main road until you reach a small lane on the left. Llansanffraid church, strangely dedicated to the Irish saint Bridget, is clearly visible ahead of you, so head straight for that as the path to Llanrhystud starts at the left of the church along an old pilgrim road. There is a second church dedicated to another female saint here – St Non whose son, St. David, was reputedly born in Llanon around 500 AD.

But back to our old pilgrim road. This gives way to a path which crosses fields after a short while, and continues through kissing gates before coming out at a group of lime kilns. This area is managed by the Wildlife Trust West Wales as an ancient monument site and wildlife nature reserve. The path continues with the kilns on your right until it reaches a stile with an arrow pointing to a footpath on your right.

Cross the stile and turn left instead, as your route now must carry on along the terraced storm beach of large pebbles. If you

Llanon

Aberaeron ⇐
(A487)

24

walk along the top 'terrace' of this beach, not only will it save you a climb back up from the beach later, but it will be easier to spot the small car-parking area. It is there that you need to leave the beach and walk along the lane until nearly reaching the main A487 and the Shell garage looming in front of you.

Just before the main road, turn left at the sign to Pencarreg Caravan Park and continue along the lane until reaching the site, which is the start of the next section of your walk.

How to get there:
A487; B4337. Regular buses to Aberystwyth and Aberaeron
Facilities: PO. Shop, pub, garage with restaurant, accommodation, Penrhos golf and leisure club with accommodation a short walk away along the B4337

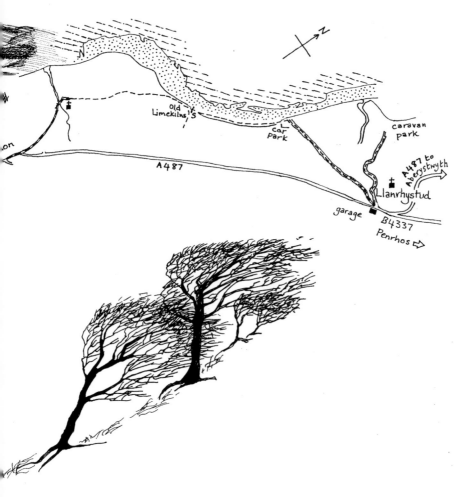

Llanrhystud to Aberystwyth
10.6 miles/17 kilometres

This long, wild stretch of coastline is one of the remotest in Ceredigion and gives stunning views of Aberystwyth and Constitution Hill. There is now a continuous coastal path thanks to a recent footpath creation between the property Mynachdy'r graig and the derelict farm building, Ffos las.

The sign-posted coast path starts at the Pencarreg Caravan site and follows the top of the touring caravan field to a stile, then continues across farmland before descending to a small wooden bridge. Crossing the bridge, the path climbs steeply and then winds its way through bracken and gorse covered slopes. In summer, this path can get quite overgrown so take extra care. The

peaceful solitude that awaits you though is well worth the effort of bashing back the bracken. The Wildlife Trust of South and West Wales reserve at Penderi is interesting; a windblown stunted oak woodland on the steep coastal slope probably of great age. This is also a good spot for watching seals on the rocks below. The path descends through the bracken covered slopes to emerge onto open flat fields. Cross the stile where it emerges and continue straight ahead across the fields with the fence line on your left. This path leads to the white-washed old farm buildings of Mynachdy'r Graig. Follow the coast path sign to the stile beyond the front of the farmhouse, and continue across the fields crossing another 4 stiles as you head

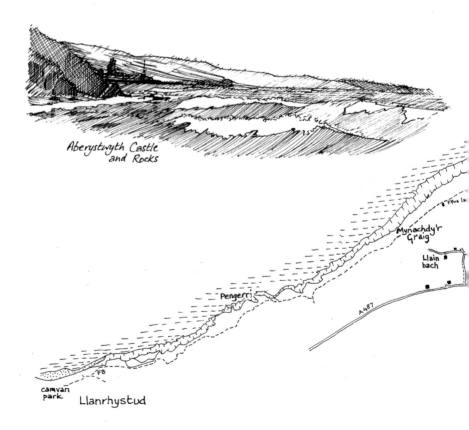

Aberystwyth Castle and Rocks

Ffos la

Mynachdy'r Graig

Llain bach

Pengerri

A487

FB

caravan park Llanrhystud

26

north along the cliff-top. At the 6th stile from Mynachdy'r, go straight ahead up the path leading up the slope to another coastpath sign that points left along a track leading down to the derelict Ffos Las. Approaching the old farm buildings, a coast path sign on the right points downwards to a track leading away to the right. This bridle way continues, climbs and passes through an old hawthorn 'arch' to where it meets at a t-junction with another track Turn right and follow this track until it emerges onto the access road to Morfa Bychan Caravan Park.

Turn left and follow the road down until you see a coastal path sign on the right. This final stretch of path into Aberystwyth offers some of the finest views of the whole of Ceredigion. Looking east from the high ridge you will see the Cambrian Mountains with the summit of Plynlimon; to the south New Quay headland and Cardigan Island; and ahead, Ceredigion's northern boundary of the Dyfi Estuary.

The path descends steeply to the long sweep of Tanybwlch beach, the best shingle beach in Ceredigion, designated a Site of Special Scientific Interest because of its distinctive plant communities. Look out for the unusual prostrate blackthorn buried deep in the shingle which is thought to be probably 200 years old. This area is now part of a Local Nature Reserve, dominated by the imposing Hill Fort of Pen Dinas and Wellington monument. Carry on walking along the beach to the harbour at Aberystwyth, the largest town in the County.

How to get there:
A487; A44; A4120. Bus and train services.
Facilities: PO. Banks. Shops. Cafes and restaurants. Accommodation. Tourist Information Centre.
Features of Interest: Arts Centre, National Library of Wales; Museum, Vale of Rheidol steam railway.

Pen Dinas

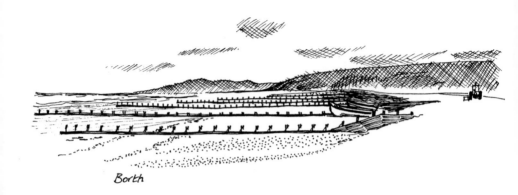

Borth

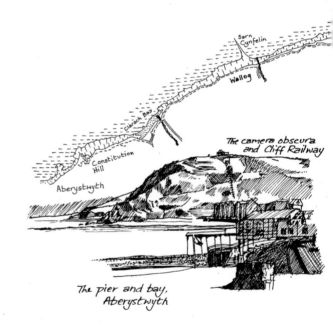

Sarn Cynfelin

Wallog

Clarach Bay

Constitution Hill

Aberystwyth

The camera obscura
and Cliff Railway

The pier and bay,
Aberystwyth

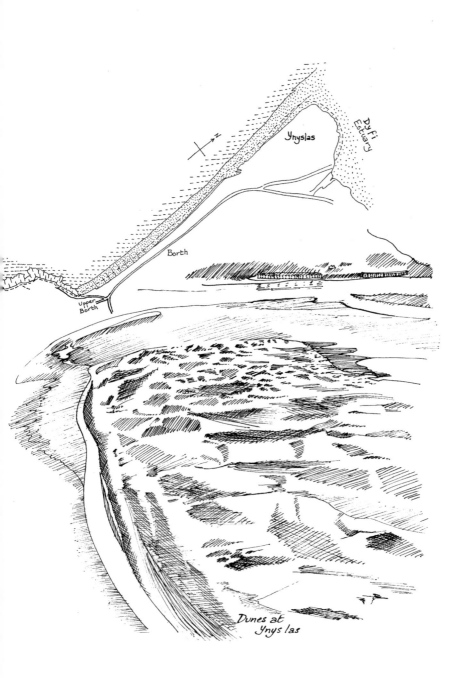

Dyfi Estuary

Ynyslas

Borth

Upper Borth

Dunes at Ynys las

Aberystwyth to Ynyslas
9.9 miles/15.8 kilometres

Coastal path all the way to Borth. Very steep stretches from Wallog, but a gentle stroll along the fine sandy beach from Borth to Ynyslas to finish.

Leave the town of Aberystwyth by the footpath leading up to Constitution Hill at the northern end of North Beach. Alternatively during the summer months, take a ride up on the clifftop railway. At the summit, there is a café and the largest Camera Obscura in the world. Follow the coastal path that passes in front of the café and continue along a well trodden path to the beach at Clarach. Clarach is a holiday village of caravans; busy in summer but quiet as the grave in the winter.

To the north of the beach by the Leisure Centre, an ancient track rises up the hill between stone and earth banks. These soft clay cliffs have become quite badly eroded in parts, but this section soon gives way to more stable terrain after Wallog. Extending from the shore at Wallog is the impressive Sarn Cynfelin. A feature unique to Cardigan Bay and part of the Pen Llyn a'r Sarnau Special Area of Conservation, this ridge is 20 metres wide and extends out below the surface of the sea for 11km. It is thought to be a morrainic feature dating from the last Ice Age. A lime kiln, recently restored, is also of interest at Wallog.

This exhilarating stretch of coastal path continues with some steep sections to the popular seaside resort of Borth. A common sight along the wayare cormorants perched on the rocks below drying their wings. Cormorants, like other seabirds, need to submerge to feed on a variety of small fish, molluscs and small crustaceans. Cormorants have wider spaced barbs on their feathers than other divers, and so can easily become waterlogged, enabling them to catch prey at much greater depths. The only snag is that, after surfacing, they have difficulty in taking off and must then perch on a rock with wings outstretched to dry out! Stretching their wings also aids digestion after a heavy meal.

The coastal path ends at the War Memorial, where there is a small car park. There are exceptionally fine views from here to the Dyfi estuary, Ynyslas and the bogland of Cors Fochno, all part of the Dyfi National Nature Reserve. The estuary is one of the most important areas for migrant waders and wildfowl in Cardigan Bay with flocks of wigeon, mallard, teal, pintail and the only flock of greenland white-fronted geese regularly occurring in Wales. Years ago it was possible to catch a steam ferryboat across to Aberdyfi from Ynyslas Point, but nowadays you have to go by road or rail to Machynlleth to cross the river.

Beyond, the Snowdonia National Park looms. Either continue along the road through the village, or at low water follow the long sandy beach to the sand-dunes at Ynyslas and journey's end.

How to get there:
B4353 from Rhydypennau or Trerddol. Bus service to Aberystwyth. Trains from Aberystwyth to Shrewsbury.
Facilities: Ynyslas Visitor Centre (seasonal). Shops, pubs, PO, accommodation, Car parks at Ynyslas (Dyfi National Nature Reserve); Borth Golf Club.
Features of interest: Stumps of a 6000 year old submerged forest of alder, pine, oak and hazel on Borth/Ynyslas beach

WELSH

The meanings of some of the commom words found in local place names

aber	mouth	**glyder**	heap	**plas**	mansion
afon	river,	**glyn**	glen	**porth**	port
	stream	**gors**	bog	**pwll**	pool
allt	hillside	**grug**	heather		
		gwen	white	**rhaeadr**	waterfall
bach	small	**gyrn**	peak	**rhiw**	hill
banc	hill			**rhos**	marsh,
blaen	head of	**hafod**	summer		moor
	valley	dwelling		**rhyd**	ford
bont	bridge	**hen**	old		
bryn	hill	**hendre**	winter	**sarn**	road
bwlch	pass	dwelling		**sych**	dry
		heol	road		
cadair	chair	**hir**	long	**tarren**	hill
caer	fort			**tomen**	mound
capel	chapel	**isaf**	lowest	**traeth**	shore,
castell	castle				beach
cefn	ridge	**llan**	church	**traws**	across
ceunant	ravine	**llech**	slate	**tref**	hamlet,
coch	red	**llidiart**	gate		home
coed	wood	**llwyd**	grey	**twll**	hole
craig	rock	**llyn**	lake	**ty**	house
croes	cross				
cwm	valley	**maen**	stone	**uchaf**	highest
		maes	field		
dinas	fort, city	**mawr**	big	**y, yr**	the, of the
dol	meadow	**melin**	mill	**ynys**	island
du	black	**moch**	pigs	**ysgol**	school
dwr	water	**moel**	bare hill	**ystrad**	valley
dyffryn	valley	**mor**	sea		floor
		mynach	monk		
eglwys	church	**mynydd**	mountain		
esgair	hillspur				
		nant	stream		
fach	small	**neuadd**	hall		
fan	high place	**newydd**	new		
fawr	large				
fechan	small	**ogof**	cave		
felin	mill				
ffordd	road	**pandy**	mill		
ffynnon	spring, well	**pant**	hollow		
foel	bare hill	**parc**	field, park		
fynydd	mountain	**pen**	top		
garth	enclosure,	**penmaen**	rocky		
hill			headland		
glas	green,	**pistyll**	waterfall,		
blue			spout		

PRONUNCIATION

These basic points should help non-Welsh speakers

Welsh	English equivalent
c	always hard, as in cat
ch	as in the Scottish word loch
dd	as th in then
f	as f in of
ff	as ff in off
g	always hard as in got
ll	no real equivalent. It is like 'th' in then, but with an 'L' sound added to it, giving 'thlan' for the pronunciation of the Welsh 'Llan'.

In Welsh the accent usually falls on the last-but-one syllable of a word: **Llanrhystud** – pronounce it 'thlan-rhu-stud' and you will be close!

KEY TO THE MAPS

----	Walk route
✗ gate	Gate
⅌	Stile
✗ SP	Sign post
FB	Foot bridge
WC	Toilets
♀ ♂	Woodland
⛪	Church

THE COUNTRYSIDE CODE

• Be safe – plan ahead and follow any signs

• Leave gates and property as you find them

• Protect plants and animals, and take your litter home

• Keep dogs under close control

• Consider other people

The CroW Act 2000, implemented throughout Wales in May 2005, introduced new legal rights of access for walkers to designated open country, predominantly mountain, moor, heath or down, plus all registered common land. This access can be subject to restrictions and closure for land management or safety reasons for up to 28 days a year. The following web site operated by Countryside Council for Wales will provide updated information on any closures.
www.ccw.gov.uk/countrysideaccesswales